WRAP YOUR HEART AROUND GOD

Shanon Crouch

ISBN 979-8-89345-050-7 (paperback)
ISBN 979-8-89345-051-4 (digital)

Copyright © 2024 by Shanon Crouch

All rights reserved. No part of this publication may be reproduced, distributed, or transmitted in any form or by any means, including photocopying, recording, or other electronic or mechanical methods without the prior written permission of the publisher. For permission requests, solicit the publisher via the address below.

Christian Faith Publishing
832 Park Avenue
Meadville, PA 16335
www.christianfaithpublishing.com

Printed in the United States of America

Preface

This book is written to help you understand how to wrap your heart around Jesus. This is my life story of how I grew to wrap my heart around Jesus. Like most of us, I accepted Jesus Christ as a child and was patted on the back and told I was good to go; so I went on with my life thinking I was good to go, only to find out that I had no idea how to live in this world. I failed over and over, trying to fit in. I did some good things and a lot of bad things. I even went to church trying to fit in, only to find out I was missing something. I knew Jesus, so what was missing?

What I have found out over the years is that this world cannot give us what our heart desires. It doesn't matter what we try to do; we just cannot fit in. Like most of you, I knew I was missing something; but I knew Jesus and was still was missing something. So in this book, I will explain what I was missing and how I got there. It is a journey that took me over sixty years to figure out. I love God and you too much to keep to myself what our Lord put on my heart to write. What I was missing was a relationship with Jesus Christ. It is through a relationship with Jesus Christ that we can have peace in this world and fit in. A relationship takes time to build and fully develop. It is only through us working on that relationship that we grow to understand what true love is—an eternal relationship walking in love in this world. I pray that you open your heart to the words our Lord Jesus put in my heart to write to you to help you wrap your arms around Jesus so you can find what you have been missing.

Show the Love

Our actions will show that we belong to the truth, so we will be confident when we stand before God. Even if we feel guilty, God is greater than our feelings and He knows everything.
—1 John 3:19–20 NLT

We should be living a life that shows the world the love of Jesus Christ in our heart—in everything we say and do—in a way that brings great honor and glory to God. If we are truly living that way, we will be able to stand before God with confidence.

What about feeling guilty? Well, there are two reasons. The first is feeling guilty because the Holy Spirit is laying in our heart, where our guilt comes from. The second comes from our self-doubt; we know we feel unworthy to stand before God.

Always remember, God knows our heart, and he has already forgiven us of our sins. So if you are living a life that brings honor and glory to God, you should not feel guilty for anything.

Rejoice in the love and mercy of our God.

Share The Grace

When I think of all this, I, Paul, a prisoner of Christ Jesus for the benefit of you Gentiles—assuming, by the way, that you know God gave me this special responsibility of extending his grace to you Gentiles. As I briefly wrote earlier, God himself revealed his mysterious plan to me. As you read what I have written, you will understand my insight into the plan regarding Christ. God did nor reveal it to previous generations, but now by his Spirit he has revealed it to his holy apostles and prophets.
—Ephesians 3:1–5 NLT

We see in God's Word that we all have the same grace that God gave to the apostles and prophets. It is extended to us. Sometimes I get overwhelmed by God's love for us. We can't do anything to earn it, and if you are like me, we don't deserve it; however, because of God's love for us, he pours his abundant grace on us.

That is why I don't understand why we don't show others the same grace. Yes, God is still there, waiting for you to extend to others that same grace he has given to you. That is our calling: to spread the good word to others as disciples.

Show The Kindness

So we tell others about Christ, warning everyone and teaching everyone with all this wisdom God has given us. We want to present them to God perfect in their relationship to Christ. That's why I work and struggle so hard, depending on Christ's mighty power that works within me.
—Colossians 1:28–29 NLT

We all need to be telling everyone about our Lord and Savior, Jesus Christ. However, we need to remember to always do it in a loving way.

This is where a lot of churches have failed in two ways. First is by forcing or scaring people to receive the good news about our Lord and Savior, Jesus Christ, when their hearts are not ready. We are here to show them the love of Jesus Christ in our hearts, not to beat or force it on them.

Second, after they have accepted Jesus Christ in their hearts, we shake their hands and say, "You are good to go. You are saved." While this is true, we should also be congratulating them and welcoming them into God's family. This is only the beginning; we need to teach them how to grow their relationship with God.

Remember, they are new believers and don't have the foundation of God's Word in their heart. We need to mentor and help teach them to read and understand God's Word so they will have a good foundation to build a strong relationship with him. They also need a strong foundation in their hearts to stand against the schemes of Satan.

As their heart grows, we can teach them how to teach and disciple others. Most churches have fallen short in this area for many years, and that is why we have seen many backslide as Christians. They were never taught to understand the Holy Spirit, who lives in them to help guide and mold them through the trials of life to be more like Jesus.

No Fear

Such love has no fear, because perfect love expels all fear. If we are afraid, it's fear of punishment, and this shows that we have not fully experienced his perfect love. We love each other because he loved us first.
—1 John 4:18–19 NLT

We have no fear because we know God is with us. We need to understand that God is not punishing us; he is using the hills and valleys in our life to mold us to be more like Jesus because of His love for us. Without God in our hearts, we cannot truly love. It is only through God living in our hearts can we love others like God loves us.

God's Promise

Dear friends, if we don't feel guilty, we can come to God with bold confidence. And we will receive from Him whatever we ask because we obey Him and do the things that please Him.
—1 John 3:21–22 NLT

We don't feel guilty if we follow God's law and commandments. That way, we are living a life that brings honor and glory to God, by showing the world the love of Jesus Christ in our hearts in everything we do and say. If we are living a godly life, God hears what we ask, and he answers our prayers because we are pleasing him in everything.

The Third Angel

Then a third angel followed then shouting. "Anyone who worships the beast and his stature or who accepts his mark on the forehead or on the hand must drink the wine of Gods cup of anger. It has been poured full strength into God's cup of wrath. And they will be tormented with fire and burning sulfur in the presence of the holy angels and the Lamb. The smoke of their torment will rise forever and ever, and they will have no relief day or night, for they have worshipped the beast and his statue and have accepted the mark of his name." This means that God's holy people must endure persecution patiently, obeying his commands and maintaining their faith in Jesus. And I heard a voice from heaven saying, "Write down: Blessed are those who die in the Lord from now on. Yes, says the Spirit, they are blessed indeed, for they will rest from their hard work; for their good deeds follow them!"
—Revelation 14:9–13 NLT

My heart is still hurting over all of this, knowing that the end is drawing near. Our country and this world are growing darker every day. Time is running out, and there are still so many lost people out there who do not know the truth. We need to be showing them that there is still good out there. We are God's children, and the light of Jesus Christ's love should be shining through us so brightly that they, too, should want what we have.

But I have to remind you what the Scriptures say: we will be attacked and persecuted, and some of us will be killed. Our faith must remain strong, remembering *God is with us."*

So my prayers are that you remain strong in our Lord Jesus Christ and continue spreading the good news about our Lord and Savior, Jesus Christ, teaching all of God's commands in a loving way.

Like always, I am sending lots of hugs and love to each one of you, and my prayers are with you.

Stay Focused

Those who are dominated by the sinful nature think about sinful things, but those who are controlled by the Holy Spirit think about things that please the Spirit. So letting your sinful nature command your mind leads to death. But letting the Spirit control your mind leads to life and peace. For the sinful nature is always hostile to God. It never did obey God's laws, and it never will. That's why those who are still under control of their sinful nature can never please God.
—Romans 8:5–8 NLT

So how do we change the way we think? We read God's Word, pray, and learn from godly teachers. However, I have learned that keeping our eyes on Jesus Christ is very important as we live in this dark world.

For me, it is like putting blinders on my eyes. That way, I am focused on what God wants me to do and say. I no longer want to do what pleases me; I want to do what pleases God. This gives me great joy and peace in my life because I am living for God and not this world.

When I followed this world, I was always worried about things and had no joy or peace in my life. I had hate for others and was miserable. I could not make anyone happy because I was not happy. We cannot change until we are willing to give up living for this world and start living for God.

I thank God that six years ago, he showed me I was the one standing in the way of having great joy and peace in my life because I wasn't allowing Jesus Christ to totally change my heart and the way I think. See, it is only by allowing Jesus Christ to come into your heart and change the way you think that the Holy Spirit is able to guide you on your path to righteousness.

Nothing Can Separate Us

I am convinced that nothing can ever separate us from God's love. Neither death nor life, neither angels nor demons, neither our fears for today nor our worries about tomorrow—not even the powers of hell can separate us from God's love. No power in the sky above or in the earth below—indeed nothing in all creation will ever be able to separate us from the love of God that is reveled in Christ Jesus our Lord.
—Romans 8:38–39 NLT

You see, even our worries and fears cannot separate us from God's love. Nothing in this world, the sky above, or even hell can separate us from the love of God that is revealed in our Lord and Savior, Jesus Christ.

It is still amazing to me how much God loves us; he created each one of us for a personal relationship with him. However, it is our own choice through free will to accept that relationship with his Son, Jesus Christ. Through that relationship, we grow in faith knowing that no matter what this world throws at us, God is with us every step of the way. That is what gives us great peace.

Trust The Holy Spirit

And the Holy Spirit helps us in our weakness. For example, we don't know what God wants us to pray for. But the Holy Spirit prays for us with groanings that cannot be expressed in words. And the Father who knows all hearts knows what the Spirit is saying, for the Spirit is saying, for the Spirit pleads for us believers in harmony with God's own will. And we know that God causes everything to work together for the good of those who love God and are called to his purpose for them. For God knew his people in advance, and he chose them to become like his son, so that his Son would be the first born among many brothers and sisters. And having chosen them, he called them to come to him. And having called them he gave them right standing with himself. And having given them right standing, He gave them His glory.
—Romans 8:26–30 NLT

There is so much here in these verses that we need to read them again. We know that the Holy Spirit is here to help us overcome this evil world on our path to righteousness. We also are told God knows our heart.

However, we are reminded that the Holy Spirit prays for us. The Holy Spirit knows what we need and pleads for us in harmony with God's own will, even if we don't see it.

God causes everything to work together for those who love God and are called according to his purpose for them.

God knew us before we were even created by him. God knows everything from our birth, when we would accept him through Jesus

Christ, what he called us to do, and the day we will take our last breath here on earth.

Our life in this world should always show the love of Jesus Christ in words and actions to bring great honor and glory to God.

Promise

Yet what we suffer now is nothing compared to the glory he will reveal to us later. For all creation is waiting eagerly for that future day when God will reveal who his children really are. Against its will, all creation was subjected to God's curse. But with eager hope, the creation looks forward to the day when it will join God's children in glorious freedom from death and decay. For we know all creation has been groaning as in the pains of childbirth right up to the present time. And we believers also groan, even though we have the Holy Spirit within us as a foretaste of future glory, for we long for our bodies to be released from sin and suffering. We, too, wait with eager hope for the day when God will give us our full rights as his adopted children, including the new bodies he has promised us. We were given this hope when we were saved. (If we already have something, we don't need to hope for it. But if we look forward to something we don't yet have, we must wait patiently and confidently.)
—Romans 8:18–25 NLT

We all live for the promise of our spiritual bodies so we don't live in sin or pain anymore. However, don't forget the two men God took up without seeing death. So we need to stop believing the lie we have been told—that it is our sinful nature. We have been born again in the Spirit, and we can live without sin: a life that is so full of showing the world the love of Jesus Christ in our hearts in everything we do and say in such a way that it brings great honor and glory to God. Then we can live a godly life here in this world, and others will see we are different and seek what we have. Bring glory to God to the point where he can take you up before death. Truly, what a blessing that day would be.

Breathing The Spirit Inside You

So you have not received a spirit that makes you fearful slaves, you received God's Spirit when He adopted you as His children. Now we call "Abba, Father." For His Spirit joins with our spirit to affirm that we are God's children. And since we are His children, we are His heirs. In fact, together with Christ we are heirs of God's glory. But if we are to share His glory, we also share in His suffering.
—Romans 8:15–17 NLT

Do you truly understand that you have the spirit of God living inside you? Most of us understand that when we accepted Jesus Christ as our Lord and Savior, God sends the Holy Spirit to come and live inside us.

However, our minds are limited in totally understanding exactly why or what the Holy Spirit does in our lives, if we allow it. The Holy Spirit is a direct communication from Jesus to us. It leads us closer to God, enhances our relationship with him, and shows love for those around us in a new way. It builds our faith so we don't fear anything that comes at us and molds us into the person God created us to be.

It is a glorious feeling to know God is with you at all times.

Are You On God's Team

Therefore, dear brothers and sisters, you have no obligation to do what your sinful nature urges you to do. For is you live by its dictates, you will die. But is through the power of the Spirit you put to death the deeds of your sinful nature, you will live. For all who are led by the Spirit of God are children of God.
—Romans 8:12–14 NLT

Plain and simple, everything we do and say, we are doing it for God or Satan. This world says there is a gray area. God's Word tells us that it's either black or white. If you truly start looking at it that way, you see the truth in everything you do and say. So if you live your life for yourself, you are working for Satan. If you are living your life for God, you are working for God. See, God's children are not selfish; they give their all to God because they are following the spirit of God. Plain and simple, it is our choice to follow ourselves or follow God. One leads to death, and the other leads to life, and both are eternal. I have chosen to accept Jesus Christ as my Lord and Savior and am following the Holy Spirit through the hills and valleys of life on my path to righteousness, which leads to eternal life.

We Are Cleansed

Therefore, since we have been made right in God's sight by faith, we have peace with God because of what Jesus Christ our Lord has done for us. Because of our faith, Christ has brought us into this place of undeserved privilege where we now stand, and we now stand, and we confidently and joyfully look forward to sharing God's glory.
—Romans 5:1–2 NLT

What a glorious reminder of what God does for us as we celebrate our Lord and Savior Jesus Christ's birthday today here on earth. These verses remind us why we celebrate this day. It's a reminder that we have peace in our hearts because of what Jesus Christ did for us on the cross. It is because of our faith that we know God is with us throughout all the hills and valleys of life, molding us to be more like our Savior, Jesus. Christ has brought us into a place of undeserved privilege, where we now stand, so that we may have great joy and confidence to share God's glory with others.

Abraham's Faith

Abraham never wavered in believing God's promises. In fact, his faith grew stronger, and in this he brought glory to God. He was fully convinced that God is able to do whatever he promises. And because of Abraham's faith, God counted him as righteous. And when God counted him as righteous, it wasn't just for Abraham's benefit. It was recorded for our benefit, too, assuring us that God will also count us as righteous if we believe in Him, the one who raised Jesus our Lord from the dead. He was handed over to die because of our sins, and he was raised to life to make us right with God.
—Romans 4:20–25 NLT

Do you truly understand that it is our faith that makes us righteous to God? When we believe that Jesus Christ died for our sins and God raised him from the dead to sit on the right side of him on the throne in heaven, God loves us so much and knows we need a helper, so God sent Jesus through the Holy Spirit to guide us on our journey on earth. That is why God counts us righteous—not because of the things we do but because of our faith in everything he does for us on our path to righteousness.

Hope And Trust

Even when there was no reason for hope, Abraham kept hoping—believing that he would become the father of many nations. For God had said to him, "That's how many descendants you will have!" And Abraham's faith did not weaken, even though, at 100 years of age, he figured his body was as good as dead—and so was Sarah's womb.
—Romans 4:18–19 NLT

This is a reminder of how strong Abraham's faith was. See, it was through Abraham's faith that he became the father of many nations. Abraham knew God would do what he said, even if he didn't understand or know how it would happen.

It doesn't matter how old we are or how weak we are. God will use us to do more than we could ever imagine. *All we have to do is believe.* Sounds simple, but for us, it's not so simple.

Always remember, without God, we are nothing. His plan and timing are always perfect.

Hold on to your faith and totally believe God knows your heart.

A Free Gift

So the promise is received by faith. It is given as a free gift. And we are all certain to receive it, whether or not we live according to the law of Moses, if we have faith like Abraham's. For Abraham is the father of all who believe. That is what the Scriptures mean when God told him, "I have made you the father of many nations." This happened because Abraham believed in God who brings back the dead back to life and creates new things out of nothing.
—Romans 4:16–17 NLT

We need to remember that it is by faith, believing in God's promises, that we receive eternal life. It is nothing we can earn, buy, or even deserve. It is by God's grace that he gives his promises to those who believe. It is by our faith that God counts us righteous. It is by faith we believe that God sent his Son, Jesus Christ, to die for our sins. It is by faith we know that we are cleansed of our sins by the blood of Jesus Christ. It is by faith we believe that God raised Jesus Christ from the dead three days later and seated him on his right side on the throne in heaven. It is by faith that we know that Jesus Christ is living inside our hearts through the Holy Spirit. See, it is by faith we know God is using the hills and valleys of this world to mold us to be more like Jesus Christ. It is by faith we know that God can use us to do more than we could ever imagine or accomplish on our own.

Relationship Of Faith

Clearly, God's promise to give the whole earth to Abraham and his descendants was based not on his obedience to God's law, but on a right relationship with God that comes by faith. If God's promise is only for those who obey the law, then faith is not necessary and the promise is pointless. For the law always brings punishment on those who try to obey it. (The only way to avoid breaking the law is to have no law to break!)
—Romans 4:13–15 NLT

We need to remember that God's law shows us that we cannot follow the law without God. It's by faith that we make our relationship with God. Our faith in God, keeping all his promises, gives us peace on this earth; and one day, through God living inside us through the Holy Spirit, we will be righteous. It is because of our love for God and through his strength that we can follow the law and his commands.

Circumcision Of The Heart

Circumcision was a sign that Abraham already had faith and that God had already accepted him and declared him to be righteous—even before he was circumcised. So Abraham is the spiritual father of those who have faith but have not been circumcised. They are counted righteous because of their faith. And Abraham is also the spiritual father of those who have been circumcised, but only is they have the same kind of faith Abraham had before he was circumcised.
—Romans 4:11–12 NLT

Circumcision is obedience to God's commands. We follow God's commands and laws because of our love for God. Faith is knowing God will fulfill all his promises to us, like eternal life with God in heaven. Faith is knowing God is with us through the hills and valleys of life, molding us to be more like Jesus on our path to righteousness. Because of our faith, we know that God can use us to do more than we could imagine; all we have to do is step out in faith and believe.

So following God's commands and laws shows God that we love him. Knowing God is with us through the trials of life and believing God can use us to do all things in faith. Faith is what makes us righteous in God's eyes; us following his commands and laws shows our love for God.

The Great Babylon

And I saw another angel flying through the sky, carrying the eternal Good News to proclaim to the people who belong to this world—to every nation, tribe, language, and people. "Fear God," he shouted. "Give glory to him. For the time has come when he will sit judge. Worship him who made the heavens, the earth, the sea, and all the springs of water." Then another angel followed him through the sky, shouting, "Babylon is fallen—that great city is fallen—because she made all nations of the world drink the wine of her passionate immortality."
—Revelation 14:6–8 NLT

This gives me great joy and sadness. Why? Because time is running out, and the end is near. I know you don't want to hear it; however, the great Babylon is us! Yes, it breaks my heart knowing this country was built on God and his commands yet has turned away from God and all his commandments. Think about it: all nations look up to us and depend on the great United States of America. People will risk their lives to get here to live without persecution.

However, we have led ourselves and them to a life of immorality and destruction. Tell me you cannot see it, and this will truly sadden my heart—not only about the loss of our great nation but all the lost people that are still out there. My heart yearns to help every one of them. However, I can't do it on my own. We have to work on this together. We must all be telling everyone about the good news about Jesus Christ in a loving way. Please do your best; time is truly running out. We want to be in heaven with all our family, friends, and even enemies. Just like Jesus Christ, our hearts must go out to all people, not just the people we love or like.

Shelter And Shadow

*Those who live in the shelter of the Most High will
find rest in the shadow of the Almighty.
This I declare about the Lord:
He alone is my refuge, my place of safety; he is my God, and I trust him.
For he will rescue you from every trap and
protect you from deadly disease.
He will cover you with his feathers. He will shelter you with his wings.
His faithful promise are your armor and protection.
Do not be afraid of the terrors of the night,
nor the arrow that flies in the day.
Do not dread the disease that stalks in the darkness,
nor the disaster that strikes at midday.*
—Psalm 91:1–6 NLT

We are under God's protection, those who have chosen to be his children. Knowing God is with us gives us peace through the hills and valleys of life. That does not mean we will not have trials and tribulations in life; it is because we know in our hearts that God is using them to mold us to be more like Jesus Christ. Knowing God is with us every step of the way to direct us through our life choices and keep us on a path of righteousness gives us great peace, even in death. God's love and faithfulness are for eternity.

What Is Wrong with Me?

Hi, my name is Shanon Crouch, and I am a faithful believer in Jesus Christ. What brought me here is a lot of things, like sex, alcohol, hate, anger, and so much more. So what is wrong with me?

Well, I have lots of problems, but let's start the story with my childhood. To be honest, I was raised on a farm and brought up to love God, this country, family, and friends. I knew Jesus Christ, and not one time did I fear death because I knew I was going to be with God in heaven. So again, I ask you, what is wrong with me, and why do I have this big hole in my heart that I can't fill?

As a young boy growing up on the farm, I was mean, really mean. Looking back, I felt like God and my family didn't love me. Now, to set the record straight, that was not the case at all; it was *me*. It was nothing my family or God did. Let me continue to explain because, thinking no one loved me, I acted out in anger. I was very mean to a lot of people, especially my mother because she was always trying to point me in the right direction; but looking back, I am so thankful for my mom not giving up on me and praying daily for me, praying that God would continue working on me to be closer to him.

Now, getting back to me. As I grew, so did my problems and the hole in my heart. Now I was covering it up with alcohol and lots of sex. I realized that I would tell girls anything they wanted to hear to get what I wanted: sex.

During this time, my grandmother lived close so we could help her after my grandpa died. One Sunday, I got a message that my grandmother's car wasn't working, and I needed to take her to church. God was continuing to use folks to get my attention; however, I wasn't listening.

Then came the time for God to take my grandmother home to be with him. I was very close to Grandmother Crouch, and the hole in my heart grew even bigger.

By this time, I was in a really dark place, and I was out of control. I even got to the point where I thought God hated me. My world was spinning out of control! It got to the point I was having blackout periods from all the alcohol, partying, and, of course, sex. God didn't give up and continued working on me. Now the hole in my heart was so big I couldn't see a way out. Then I was dating three women, and they all knew each other. And each thought I was going to marry her.

Just then, God sent another woman into my life, and her name is Amy. I truly thank God for her now, even though I did not see it then. At that time, she helped me give up alcohol, and we started going to church. We have two beautiful children that I thank God for daily. Like most families with children, jobs, and the world, Amy's and my problems grew. We started having more and more differences. We tried counseling; however, it wasn't working because I was blaming her for everything. I never admitted I had a problem. I was still not drinking, but I was giving in to my sexual desires. The hole in my heart continued to grow as my hate for her was at a dangerous point. I stayed away from the children, and finally, we got to the point where we hated each other and gave up. Then came the divorce.

I started going back to church, looking for something to fill the hole after the divorce. My children really did not want to have anything to do with me because of the divorce. Looking back, they had every right to feel that way. I was a terrible dad. I worked all the time to give them what I thought they wanted. Now I realize it was time and real love with me they wanted. So again, what is wrong with me? Why the *big* hole in my heart?

I was on Facebook, and a little blonde caught my eye. Later, I realized the blonde was really a brunette. I remembered her from high school, and I was scared of her. I finally met her, and it was just like in high school; all my fantasies were coming true.

It didn't take long until I was back to drinking and partying like a rock star. I married her, thinking I'd change her. It was too late. I was back in my dark place, and like always, that hole was continuing to get bigger. My relationship with her would give me some great stepchildren and grandchildren.

Once again, God didn't give up on me! I got up early in the morning, around six thirty, and made myself a drink. It happened to be a 1.75-liter bottle of Jose Cuervo Margarita. Anyway, it was empty by 10:30 a.m. Yes, in four hours, I drank the whole bottle. Then I was angry because I was not feeling anything—no buzz—and that hole in my heart was still there. So again I asked myself, what is wrong with me?

God was still working on me, and I went through the house and dumped out all of the alcohol. Let's just say this didn't go well with her. I told her things needed to change. She told me I was the one with a problem. At the time, she was right, even though I thought it was all her.

That has been over three and a half years ago, and I have no desire to drink at all, thank God. But the deep, big hole was still in my heart. Again, God is working on me, and this time I started listening. Yes, he laid it in my heart to go to Church. The minute I walked into the church, I felt God's love, even though I was not ready for it or welcomed it yet. I sat on the back left side, hiding from everyone. In reality, that is like an elephant hiding behind a little fence. I stuck out like a sore thumb. The church and God continued to love on me. I then began to open up to some groups and pray all the time for God to save my marriage. I loved that woman so much, but I could no longer live that way. The divorce happened, and I gave her more than she asked for just to get her out of my life. Doesn't make sense when you love someone. However, God was still working on me.

A person asked me to go on a discipleship walk because I had been through the four steps at the church and was now asking for membership. I acknowledged them; there was a second and a third person, and I wrote a check. All I will say is it brought me closer to

God and reminded me that I was to stop drinking and go into the ministry. That's another story.

Looking back right now, something changed; that giant hole in my heart began to get smaller and continues to. My relationship with family has gotten better. I thank God for using my brother-in-law to call me four years ago and tell me what a piece of crap I was. I figure that is what it took for me to start crawling out of the hole I had made.

Later, I was coming back from visiting my sister and her husband at their house. I asked God to show me through his eyes what he wanted me to see. I truly meant it, but I thought God was going to show me what everybody else was doing wrong, especially my ex-wife. Well, once again, I was wrong. It was all about me. I ended up in a ditch, crying like a baby in the fetal position. Please don't pray this when driving; it can be dangerous.

It was late when I got home, yet I wrote letters to all my family. I took a bottle of water and poured it into a cup to mix with half a bottle of sleeping pills and prayed to God again to forgive me for all my sins. I also told him I was tired of failing him, my family, and friends. I was ready to come home because I was tired of sinning.

I felt God grab my shoulders and tell me I couldn't come home because I still had hate in my heart. I told God I don't hate anybody.

He said, "Yes, you do. Your ex-wife. You need to apologize to her for how you handled yourself because you claim to be a Christian."

I told God, "She will chew me up and spit me out [to say the least]." Then I realized I had no right to argue with God. So the next day, I set off to her house and told her I was wrong for everything I had done. Yes, she not only ripped out my heart but also stomped it to pieces. As I headed out to my truck with my heart torn out and my tail between my legs, I was talking to God, telling God, "I told you what was going to happen." I guess it was what I deserved and much more. It doesn't matter what she had done; it only mattered what I had done because I was a Christian. Anyway, I climbed into the truck and started to leave, and something happened. It's like someone breaking an egg on your head, and it just starts sinking down on your face. It was true peace, a peace I have never had and a peace I never want to lose.

So what is wrong with me? Why was there a huge hole in my heart? The answer is, I never gave my will over to Jesus Christ and let him be the Lord of my life. That is the only way to fill your heart with pure love. I was missing the relationship with Jesus Christ. I was missing God's love to fill that hole I made.

My prayer is that you accept Jesus Christ as your Savior and let him be the Lord of your life. Only then will you have the love to fill that hole in your heart.

> Love is patient and kind. Love is not jealous or boastful or rude. It does not demand its own way. It is not irritable and keeps no record of being wronged. It does not rejoice above injustice but rejoices whenever the truth wins out. Love never gives up, never loses faith, is always hopeful and endures through every circumstance. (1 Corinthians 13:4–7 NLT)

Thank you for giving me your time and attention. Only through the love of Jesus Christ can we change.

Lying Tongues

Beware of false prophets who come disguised as harmless sheep but are really vicious wolves. You can identify them by their fruit, that is, by the way they act. Can you pick grapes from thorn bushes, or figs from thistles? A good tree produces good fruit, and a bad tree produces bad fruit. A good tree can't produce bad fruit, and a bad tree can't produce good fruit. So every tree that does not produce good fruit is chopped down and thrown into the fire. Yes, just as you can identify a tree by its fruit, so you can identify people by their actions.
—Matthew 7:15–20 NLT

We are reminded that we need to watch out for false prophets (people). They tell us what our ears want to hear and lead us down a dark path that leads to death. Look, Satan knows he cannot come straight at you because you would recognize him and push him back; the truth is Satan just inches into our lives over time, and before we know it, we are going down the wrong path again.

So we have to be careful of all people. We all have seen Satan use people to lead others down the wrong path. All I am saying is that if you are looking up to God instead of people, you won't go down the wrong path. You will be able to see what Satan is doing to inch his way back into your life and ask God to protect you.

Not To Judge

Do not judge others, and you will not be judged. For you will be treated as you treat others. the standard you use in judging is the standard by which you will be judged. And why worry about a speck in your friend's eye when you have a log in your own? How can you think of saying to your friend. Let me help you get rid of that speck in your eye, when you can't see past the log in your own eye? Hypocrite! First get rid of the log in your own eye: then you will see well enough to deal with the speck in your friend's eye.
—Matthew 7:1–5 NLT

We are reminded not to judge others; there is only one judge that counts, and that is Jesus Christ. I know personally I have enough to answer for with what I've said and done. So don't go running around being critical about others; instead, worry about straightening out your own life first. Then you can help others in a loving way.

Remember, none of us are perfect, and we all need help. However, we should always do it in a loving way. We should be lifting every person up, not pushing them down. I don't care if it's your family or your enemies; we are to show all people the love of Jesus in our heart in everything we do and say in a way that brings great honor and glory to God.

The Hidden City

You are the salt of the earth. But what good is salt if it has lost its flavor? Can you make it salty again? It will be thrown out and trampled underfoot as worthless. You are the light of the world—like a city of a hilltop that cannot be hidden. No one lights a lamp then puts it under a basket. Instead, a lamp is placed on a lamp stand, where it gives light to everyone in the house. In the same way, let your good deeds shine out for all to see, so everyone will praise your heavenly Father.
—Matthew 5:13–16 NLT

I was once like this, the person who went to church and claimed to be a Christian on Sunday. I acted just like a good Christian man, but the rest of the week, my heart and lips were far from God. I was running from God.

I hurt a lot of people during that time and truly repented to God and the ones I had hurt. I still thank God for not giving up on me and having my sister's husband, Brian Mayo, call me and tell me what a piece of crap I was, to say it nicely. But he reminded me he was doing it because he cared about me and God cared enough for me, even though I had given up on myself.

I thank God for growing me into the man I am today, using me to show others God's love through my testimonies and allowing me to be a little light in this dark world.

Live For God

Then Jesus said to His disciples, "If any of you wants to be my follower, you must give up your own way, take up your cross, and follow me. If you try to hand on your life, you will lose it. But if you give up your life for my sake, you will save it. And what do you benefit if you gain the whole world but lose your own soul? Is anything worth more than your soul."
—Matthew 16:24–26 NLT

When you truly follow Jesus Christ, you realize that you want his will for your life, not your own. We no longer want what this world wants; instead, we want what God wants for our life.

It's no more about us; it's about others and showing God's love.

Our relationship with God is so strong we would rather face death than submit to this world.

Either way, it is a win for us. In death, we will be home with God for eternity; and if we continue living, we have more time to tell everyone about our Lord and Savior, Jesus Christ.

Live for God

Then he said to crowd, "If any of you wants to be my followers, you must give up your own way, take up your cross daily, and follow me. If you try to hang on to your own life, you will lose it. But if you give up your life for my sake, you will save it. And what do you benefit if you gain the whole world but are yourself lost or destroyed? If anyone is ashamed of me and my message, the Son of Man will be ashamed of that person when he returns in his glory and in the glory of the Father and the holy angels. I tell you the truth, some standing here right now will not die before they see the kingdom of God."
—Luke 9:23–27 NLT

A lot of people don't fully understand this: God gives us free will, so we have the choice to make our own decisions. Like the choice we have to accept Jesus Christ as our Lord and Savior, that is what makes it a true relationship. As we grow, we learn to choose God's will for our life, instead of our will. We realize that his way is better than our way. We no longer worry about anything because we know God is in control of everything; he has us in his hands to guide and protect us. That gives us great peace.

He then goes on to remind us that if we choose to chase this world, we will lose our life, and if we are ashamed of Jesus Christ and his message, Jesus Christ will be ashamed of us.

I have chosen Jesus Christ, and I pray you have too.

Others Come First

*Jesus replied, "What does the law of Moses say? How do you real it?"
The man answered, "You must love the Lord your God
with all your heart, all your soul, all your strength, and
all your mind. and, Love your neighbor as yourself."
"Right!" Jesus told him. "Do this and you will live!"*
—Luke 10:26–28 NLT

We know we are to love God with all our heart, body, mind, and soul; but we have a hard time loving others, especially those who have hurt us. However, here Jesus reminds us that if we love others as ourselves, we will live. If we truly do everything in love, we will live a good life; if we don't, we won't. It is your choice how you live.

    I chose to live in love in everything that I do and speak in such a way that I brings great honor and glory to God. That is how we show God how much we love him—by showing others love.

Accept This

Then he said to his disciples, "Anyone who accepts your message is also accepting me. And anyone who rejects you is also rejecting me. And anyone who rejects me is rejecting God, who sent me."
—Luke 10:16 NLT

We are all called to spread the good news about our Lord and Savior, Jesus Christ, in a loving way. Keep in mind that we are called to be his disciples. We should show the world we are his disciples not only by what we say but also by the things we do every day. See, people of this world should see the love of Jesus Christ in our hearts in everything we do and say, in such a way that it brings great honor and glory to God. That way, they will come to you and ask you what is different. Why do you show kindness and love?

Just remember, if someone does not like you because you follow Jesus Christ, they are not only rejecting you; they are also rejecting God. Remember, we will not be accepted by all the people of this world because we are not of this world; we belong to God.

Nail It To The Cross And Leave It There

Those who belong to Christ Jesus have nailed the passions and desires of their sinful nature to his cross and crucified them there. Since we are living by the Spirit, let us follow the Spirit's leading in every part of our lives.
—Galatians 5:24–25 NLT

We are being reminded that we need to nail our sinful desires to the cross and crucify them there. What God's Word is saying is to nail them at the cross and leave them there. Stop going over there and picking them back up. Jesus paid your debt in full. Let it go.

Now that we are living by the Spirit, we should be following the Spirit in every part of our lives. Not some of the time but all the time. We should be living a life that shows the world the love of Jesus Christ in our hearts in everything we do and say, to bring great honor and glory to God.

One God

*For there is one body and one Spirit, just as you have
been called to one glorious hope in the future.
There is one Lord, one faith, one baptism, One God and
Father of all, who is over all, in all, and living through all.*
—Ephesians 4:4–6 NLT

There is only one God who created everything in this whole universe, who created you and me and gave us the breath of life. He loves us so much that he created each one of us for a personal relationship with him.

However, because of our sinful nature, we are in the dark. Again, I tell you God loves us so much that he will make us clean through his Son, Jesus Christ, when we accept him as our Savior. When we accept Jesus, we are forgiven. Then we receive the Holy Spirit to help us grow our relationship with God through the Bible, prayers, and faith. Yes, there will be hills and valleys in life; God will use these to mold us into the purpose he has for our life.

We have great peace knowing we have God with us through our journey on earth.

Rebuilding From the Inside

Through I am the least deserving of all God's people, he graciously gave me the privilege of telling the Gentiles about the endless treasures available to them in Christ. I was chosen to explain to everyone this mysterious plan that God, the Creator of all things, had kept secret from the beginning.
—Ephesians 3:8–10 NLT

I know I feel the same way, really. For years, I claimed to be a Christian and was even boastful about it. Yet I was so far from God. I hurt a lot of people by what I said and did. Thankfully, God gave me his mercy and grace to break down my prideful heart and bring me to my knees, humbling me. He did this for me, to rebuild me with the loving heart that I have today.

I feel like I am a Saul when he was working on becoming Paul, and that's because I am a long way from being like Jesus. However, I know I am going in the right direction because I am seeing God using me to do his good works every day.

This was his plan long ago. God created each one of us for a special relationship with him. He also gave us free will to choose. We have the choice to serve Satan or God. He will put people and roadblocks in your life to guide you to him because he loves you and wants a real relationship with you.

So I want to ask you, is today the day you choose to have an eternal relationship with God and see all the endless treasures he has in store for you?

Equal Inheritance

And this is God's plan: Both Gentiles and Jews who believe the Good News share equally in the riches inherited by God's children. Both are part of the same body and both enjoy the promise of blessings because they belong to Christ Jesus. By God's grace and mighty power, I have been give the privilege of serving him by spreading this Good News.
—Ephesians 3:6–7 NLT

We are now children of God because we have accepted Jesus Christ as our Lord and Savior, so we have all God's grace and promises. I still think we have already been blessed with the best gift of all: *eternal life with God*; everything else is just God's abundant blessings. Yes, it is not easy being a Christian; however, having the great love and peace we experience knowing God is with us every step is better than anything else we can imagine.

I also want to remind you we are God's disciples, so we need to continue to show this world the love of Jesus Christ shining in our hearts in everything we do and say, in such a way that brings great honor and glory to God. We should be telling others all that God has done in our life and about the good news of Jesus our Lord and Savior.

More than You Guess

Now all glory to God, who is able, through his mighty power at work within us, to accomplish infinitely more than we ask or think. Glory to him in the church and in Christ Jesus through all generations forever and ever! Amen.
—Ephesians 3:20–21 NLT

We are reminded through God's mighty power working in us that he can use us to do more than we can think or even imagine. God uses us to do amazing things through him. However, sometimes God is waiting for us to take that first step of faith, knowing he is with us. Have you ever wondered why the church and our community are lacking in getting some things done? It's because of several reasons. First, they are waiting to be asked personally because they don't have the faith to make the first step. Second, they think they are too busy; all that shows me is that their faith is weak because all things are possible through the strength of God in us. Lastly, they are just happy being a benchwarmer on Sunday. They give God praises one day a week, and then they walk out of the church and continue to do the things of this world.

Truly, I say to you, if you are God's child, you will do what God has called you to do, and it's not because you have to but because of your love for him. If you love God, you have love for all people, not just your family and friends. All people should see the love of God in your heart in everything you do and say.

The Creator

When I think of all this, I fall to my knees and pray to the Father, the Creator of everything in heaven and on earth. I pray that from his glorious, unlimited resources he will empower you with inner strength through his Spirit. Then Christ will make his home in your hearts as you trust in him. Your roots will grow down into God's love and keep you strong. And may you have the power to understand, as all God's people should, how wide, how long, how high, and how deep his love is. May you experience the love of Christ, though it is too great to understand fully. Then you will be made complete with all fullness of life and power that comes from God.
—Ephesians 3:14–19 NLT

These verses still humble me and bring me to my knees. Really think about it. Our God, who created everything in heaven and on earth, created you and me to have an eternal relationship with him just because of his love for us. This brings great tears of joy to my heart because I will be spending eternity with you, my fellow believers, whom I love so much, in heaven.

God loves us so much that he made a way for us to have a relationship with him, even though we were still full of sin, by sending his Son, Jesus Christ, to die on the cross to wash away our sins with his blood. God did not stop there; three days later, God raised Jesus Christ to sit on the right side of his throne to show us he has power over death. He did this so we can have eternal life. God did not stop there either; he also sent the Holy Spirit to help us through the hills and valleys of life to grow us to be more like his Son, Jesus Christ. And through the Holy Spirit, we grow complete with all the fullness of life and power that comes from God.

Come To Him

Because of Christ and our faith in him, we can now come boldly and confidently into God's presence. So please don't lose heart because of my trails here. I am suffering for you, so you should feel honored.
—Ephesians 3:12–13 NLT

This reminds us that we are his children and can come to him in confidence in all things. We should truly come to him in all things. How many times do we do something on our own and realize afterward that we should have reached out to God first? Not just the big things but the little ones too. If we truly want to live godly lives in this dark world, we need to bring everything before God.

Just like in the valleys in life, we should not lose faith because we know God is with us as he is molding us to be like his Son, Jesus. So instead of having our own little pity party, we should be praising God for loving us so much that he wants a deeper relationship with us.

It is through these times we grow the most. Think about this: when we are on top of the hills of life, how much do we really reach out and praise God? It is when we are in the valleys that we reach out to him. God is there all the time, and he wants us to be there with him all the time. Nobody wants a part-time relationship. They want a deep, meaningful relationship.

So my question today is, are you going to stop having a part-time relationship and go for a deeper, full-time relationship with God and your Savior, Jesus Christ?

We Are The Church

God's purpose in all this was to use the church to display his wisdom in its rick variety to all the unseen rules and authorities in the heavenly places. This was his eternal plan, which he carried out through Christ Jesus our Lord.
—Ephesians 3:10–11 NLT

We have to understand we are the church (not a building). Each one of us is a building block for God's church, and Jesus Christ is the cornerstone on which the church is built. This is what brings honor to God when we do what he is calling us to do. See, God created each one of us to do a special job for his kingdom, and when we follow God's will and do it, he rejoices. However, we all have been called to spread the good news about Jesus Christ by the way we live in this earthly world. It is by the world seeing the change in our life since we have accepted Jesus Christ as our Lord and Savior that brings them to us (that is what will draw them to us), wanting to know what changed in our life. Don't worry about what you have to say; the Holy Spirit will give you the words they need to hear at that moment. Just be willing to step out in faith for the glory of God.

Our Lord Jesus has put it in my heart to write about the Holy Spirit and how important it is for us to listen and follow the Holy Spirit so we can grow to be more like Jesus.

Baptized By Water

After his baptism, as Jesus came out of the water, the heavens were opened, and he saw the spirit of God descending like a dove on him. And a voice from heaven said, "This is my dearly loved son, who brings me great joy."
—Matthew 3:16–17 NLT

John answered their questions by saying, "I baptize you with water, but someone is coming soon who is greater than I am—so much greater that I am not even worthy to be his slave and untie the straps of his sandals. He will baptize you with the Holy Spirit and with fire."

So why did the Holy Spirit fall on Jesus like a dove, and why does Jesus baptize us with the Holy Spirit and with fire? Well, the first is easy to explain: Jesus was innocent, without any sin. So God gave him the Holy Spirit in the form of a dove. The Holy Spirit was given to him by God to give him power and strength to encourage him to finish what he was sent to accomplish in this world.

This is the second part: God sent Jesus Christ to live in us through the Holy Spirit the very second we accepted Jesus Christ as our Lord and Savior. Now it comes upon us as fire to start by purifying our hearts from our sins. As we listen and follow the Holy Spirit, we start overcoming the sins in our lives. We feel guilty when we sin because we want God to be proud of us; that way, we can become more like Jesus. We still must do our part by growing the relationship through reading God's Word, praying, and listening to the Holy Spirit.

The Holy Spirit gives us more and more understanding of God's Word so we have the strength to overcome the sins of this world and help our faith grow. We can do more than we could ever imagine, doing our part to grow God's kingdom.

Brothers and sisters, it is only through the Holy Spirit that we can overcome the sins of this dark world. As we grow in faith, we accomplish things we never knew we had the strength to do. It is only through the Holy Spirit that we can become more like Jesus and glorify our Heavenly Father. My prayers are that you are studying God's Word, praying, and listening to the Holy Spirit living inside you so that you become more like Jesus and have the faith to do more than you could ever imagine in your part to grow the kingdom of God.

A Sign From Paul

That night the Lord appeared to Paul and said, "Be encouraged, Paul. Just as you have been a witness to me here in Jerusalem, you must preach the Good News in Rome as well."
—Acts 23:11 NLT

It is amazing that our Lord Jesus appeared to Paul to encourage him and tell him that he would preach the good news in Rome, like he did in Jerusalem. I want you to know that the Holy Spirit living inside Paul is also the one living inside of you. So why can't we do all that Paul does? Plain and simple, our faith is too weak to take the first step in faith. See, our Lord Jesus told Paul to do something, and he stepped out in faith and did it. Paul stepped out in faith knowing that our Lord Jesus would carry him through whatever he called him to do. Our problem today is our love for our Lord Jesus has not fully matured, so our faith is weak—period. We are more worried about what others might think or say, so we make up excuses why we can't do it. I want you to ask yourself this question: Is God telling you, you can't do it, or is it Satan telling you, you can't do it? You know the answer! I have told you all before our Lord Jesus is not going to call you to do something you know you cannot do. No, he is calling you to do something you know you can't do without Him.

My prayer is that you step out in faith, knowing our Lord Jesus will be with you every step of the way to what he is calling you to do.

Let Him Lead

Everyone who believes that Jesus is the Christ has become a child of God. And everyone who loves the father loves his child, too. We know we love God's children if we love God and obey his commandments.
—1 John 5:1–2 NLT

Everyone who has accepted Jesus Christ as their Lord and Savior is a child of God. Everyone who loves God the Father loves his children and shall obey his commandments. God tells us we should love one another—period, so why do we have a hard time doing this simple thing? It has taken me many years to get to the place, to walk in love every day. I now have love for all people, especially the lost. I want them all to know Jesus Christ is their Lord and Savior. I understand they are like I used to be, filled with hate and misunderstanding. I did not know how to love. Why? Because I accepted Jesus Christ's salvation, but I did not let Jesus into my heart to change the way I thought. We all have a hard time giving our control over to God. We like to be in control; we all struggle with that. When we finally invite Jesus Christ into our heart and are willing to let him change us, that is when truly we can love all people. We also receive something just as special: true peace in our life. That comes from knowing that no matter what this world throws at us, Jesus Christ is with us every step of the way for eternity. That true peace cannot come from another source. It is so special that you never want to lose it, and you will give up everything to keep it.

My prayers are that you have accepted Jesus Christ and are willingly allowing him to come into your heart and change the way you think, so you can love all people, especially the lost. And because of that relationship, you have great peace in your life knowing Jesus Christ is with you every step of the way for eternity.

Material Things

Do not love this world nor the things it offers you, for when you love the world, you do not have the love of the Father in you. For the world offers only a craving for physical pleasure, a craving for everything we see, and pride in our achievements and possessions. These are not from the Father but are from the world. And this world is fading away, along with everything that people crave. But anyone who does what pleases God will live forever.
—1 John 2:15–17 NLT

We should not desire the things of this world, yet we do it all the time. We lust for careers, cars, houses, money, power, drugs, sinful love, and alcohol. We think it's okay because the world says it's okay. It is so sad to see what the world has become. I am so heartbroken. Satan has blinded so many people from seeing the truth. Everything we have been taught, what is good, is now bad, and evil is now good. I am sad because a lot of people are going to spend eternity in hell because they believe what the world is telling them.

The ones who truly know God know that this world will come to an end one day and that time is running out. We have peace knowing God is in control. We still need to continue to study God's Word and do a lot of praying until he takes us home. We can stand strong in our faith while this world continues to get eviler. What can we do? We need to continue being a light in this dark world, with no strings attached, showing that someone really loves them for who they are. We need to show our fellow man what true love is. If we can just have one more person see the love of Jesus Christ in us and they, too, can choose to accept Jesus Christ as their Lord and Savior, we have done what God has called us to do, and that is to be disciples.

My prayer is that you continue being strong in your faith and continue being the light in the dark world, spreading the gospel, so that when the opportunity arises, God will, through you, spread the good news to others.

Apostle Predict

But you, my dear friends, must remember what the apostles of our Lord Jesus Christ predicted. They told you that in the last times there would be scoffers whose purpose in life is to satisfy their ungodly desires. These people are the ones who are creating division among you. They follow their natural instincts because they do not have God's spirit in them.
—Jude 17–20 NLT

We are being reminded of what the end of time will be like. These people only care about themselves, and we are seeing more and more of this every day. They are now telling us that good is evil and evil is good. They are telling us we are narrow-minded and need to change our way of thinking. They are wrong; we are God's children, and we are commanded to love everyone. We are to hate the sin that is in them but not the sinner. I am also reminded that we, too, were like this before our relationship with Jesus Christ, and we will continue to battle ourselves with the sin that is still in us. We truly should have mercy and show them grace, just like Jesus Christ does for you. I'm telling all of you this because time is running out, and tomorrow is not promised. I want all of you to be in heaven with me, and I know you do too. Please continue showing your love for God to all people by telling them about our Lord and Savior, Jesus Christ. We don't want to miss one opportunity God gives us to spread the good news in the end times.

My brothers and sisters, my prayer is that you'll be strong in your faith and be a shining light in this dark world, telling as many people as you can about how much Jesus Christ loves them and how he changed your life.

Chew This

I got up to go to work like normal, but instead of putting a chew of tobacco in my mouth, I put it in my pocket. I climbed into my truck to go to work. When I got to work, I pulled the tobacco out of my pocket and laid it on the seat. I did not think about it at all. About an hour later, one of our customers came in and asked me for a chew of Levi Garrett. I had been chewing Levi Garrett for a lot of years. I told our customer he could have my tobacco and that it was lying on the seat of my truck because I didn't chew tobacco anymore. He left to go get the tobacco, and my brother asked me, "What do you mean, you don't chew tobacco anymore?"

I looked at him and told him, "I don't chew tobacco anymore."

At that time, I did not think much more about it. I finished my day at work and went home, fixed dinner for the family, and went to bed.

That night, I had a vision. God was telling me that he was calling me to his ministry. But he wanted me to stop drinking. I had to do it for God to show I was ready to serve him. God told me he took away my desire to chewing tobacco to show me he was real. God also told me that he would not take the desires to drink away because he wanted me to do it because of my love and my desire to serve him.

Testify

And this is what God testified: He has given us eternal life, and this life is in his son. Whoever has the son has life; whoever does not have God's son does not have life.
—1 John 5:11–12 NLT

The Lord of my life tells us in his Word, there is only one way to have eternal life, and that is through his Son, Jesus Christ! There is no other road to be saved and live eternally. So, brethren, if you are in church and they're telling you can get to heaven by doing good deeds, buying your way in, or doing anything else, do not believe them. They are leading you down the wide and broad gate that leads to destruction, and there are many who go in by it. You will have an eternal separation from the Prince of Peace. I love you way too much not to tell you the truth.

My prayer is that you have accepted Jesus Christ as your Lord and Savior and are working on growing your relationship with God through Jesus Christ by reading God's Word, praying, and listening to the Holy Spirit. They will guide you on a path that leads to righteousness and eternal life. We have been given the spirit of Jesus through God. We have been implanted with Jesus Christ's seed for mercy and grace for others. You just have to accept the facts and follow the commands of the Bible. Read Psalms to see how you are expected to live.

Unexpected Blessings

It was a normal day when I left my house early to go to church to serve coffee. I was there like normal for all three services, enjoying the time fellowshipping with other believers. I left the church and was heading home. I had just gotten down the road a little bit when I saw a man walking on the side of the road. I noticed he had no sign and nothing really special about him at all. Then I heard God speak to me; he told me to turn around and give him the money I had. I stopped my truck and backed into the clearing up to the man. I got my wallet out, pulled out all the money in it, and rolled down the window to give it to him. As soon as the window rolled down, the man started praying over me. My eyes started pouring out tears; I thought I was blessing this man. Instead, he was blessing me. After he finished praying over me, I handed him the money, and he walked to the back of my truck. I looked in my rearview mirror to see if it was clear to go, and I noticed the man was nowhere to be found. I looked around, and there was no place for the man to even go; he just disappeared. That is when I realized it was an angel from God who bless me on the ministry I was about to be called to.

I realize that God still sends angels to pray over us and watch over us. That brings great tears of joy to me even to this day, knowing God loves us this much.

See God At Work

My ex called me over to take out her trash. By the time I got there and loaded up the trash, I looked at the clock, and it was 4:45 p.m. I told her I had to go before the dump closed at 5:00 p.m. So off to the dump I went, down this road to the next, and I flew right by the dump.

I said, "Lord, what do you want me to see?"

Out in front of me, to the left, was a woman standing by her car. She was talking on the cell phone and had a flat tire. I pulled up to her and asked if she needed help. She was crying and only said the tire was a flat and that the people who could help her were at home. I told her I would change the tire for her. So I opened the trunk of her car, got the spare and the jack out of the car, jacked up the car, removed the flat tire, and installed the spare. I put the flat tire and the jack back into her trunk. She offered to pay me, and I told her to keep her money.

"Just give me a hug and thank God," I said.

Well, I left feeling good and got to the light at the dump to turn around to go home because I knew that after all this time, the dump was closed. I looked over at the dump and said, "Thank you, God, for keeping the dump open." Then I looked back at the clock again; it said 4:45 p.m. I started crying; despite all the time I spent changing the tire, not one minute had elapsed. Yes, God still stops time.

Always The Same

Jesus Christ is the same yesterday, today, and forever. So do not be attracted by strange, new ideas. Your strength comes from God's grace, not from rules about food, which don't help those who follow them. We have an altar from which the priests in the Tabernacle have no right to eat.
—Hebrews 13:8–10 NLT

Jesus Christ is the same yesterday, today, and forever. Jesus Christ is our rock and our salvation. We should not let what this world thinks or says get in the way of our relationship with God through his Son, Jesus Christ. God created us to seek and follow him, not this world. God gives us our strength through the Holy Spirit to overcome this world. We should be relying on God, not this world. Man will let you down every time, but God never will. Everything we do or say should show this world the love of Jesus Christ living inside our heart. Everything we say and do should show others the great honor and love we have for God. That way, we know we are doing everything to please God, and then we will always be ready when God calls us home.

My prayer is that you follow, meditate on his words, and commit them to memory so that when you are faced by a false prophet, you will know the truth. We need to live a Christlike life by showing people the love of Jesus Christ living inside our heart so everything we say and do acknowledges the love God has for others.

What is God

Yes, they know God, but they wouldn't worship him as God or even give him thanks. And they began to think of foolish ideas of what God was like. As a result, their minds became dark and confused. Claiming to be wise, they instead became utter fools. And instead of worshipping the glorious, ever living God, they worshipped idols made to look like mere people and birds and animals and reptiles.
—Romans 1:21–23 NLT

We should speak from the heart and worship God by giving him praises constantly. But we don't. This is sorrowful but true. We put everything and anything before God. Personally, in my past, I idolized cash, my career, football, and even my wife before God. At a time, yes, I was living for my own selfish pleasures instead of living for God. I had okay days and not-so-okay days when I was living for the world. Most of the time, I was miserable and had no stillness or calm. It did not matter what I did, how much money I had, or how well my football team played. I was still trying to fill a void with worldly, superficial things. We have all been there. Some people are still chasing after the material things of this world when we should be chasing after the Messiah and trying to live a godly life, being an example and light to others to let them know they can also share in the inheritance God has promised. He has set a place for us in our Father's house.

Do you really want joy, peace, and love in your heart? Start by giving God the honor, glory, time, and praises every day instead of just on Sundays. Start living as a model that shows this world the love of Jesus Christ pouring out you. Allow everything you do to show great honor and glory to God. Please know you could have that abundant life and great peace and live on the promises of God to you. If you abide in him, you will, and for the last six years, I have been living proof. If you allow the Holy Spirit to direct your path, the better your circumstances will be.

My prayer is that you are living a life that brings honor, glory, and praises every day to God by showing this world the love of Jesus Christ living inside your heart and in everything you do and say.

You Can't have It Both Ways

If someone says, quote I love God, end quote but hates a fellow believer, that person is a liar, for if we don't love people we can see, how can we love God, whom we cannot see? And he has given us this command; Those who love God must also love their fellow believers.
—1 John 4:20–21 NLT

I don't understand how someone who claims to be a Christian says he hates a fellow believer. Thank God, Jesus Christ does not think that way. He died for all of us, not just the ones he likes. In John 13:1–5, we read about Jesus telling us that he loved all his disciples and even washed their feet to show them his love. We don't think much about it because it is easy to show love to someone you love. It is far more difficult and important to show love to someone who has hurt or betrayed you. It's easy to love nice or kind people. Being kind to bad people is the mission. They are the ones who really need the love of God. People got that way for a reason—a hurt, sin, or mistrust. Keep in mind that Jesus washed Judas Iscariot's feet even though he knew he would betray him. Jesus knew the Jewish leaders would lead him to be crucified on the cross and to his death. This had to happen for God's prophecy to come true. Remember, Jesus said he loved all his disciples, and that included Judas. Brothers and sisters, that is love and how we should love one another. God does not like the sin in us, but that does not stop him from loving us. The last time I checked, I was not without any sin, and I am sure you are not without sin either. Love one another like God loves you, because of your love for God, not because it is God's command.

My prayer is that you love all people like Jesus Christ loves you, in such a way that it honors and glorifies God. Then you will have great peace in your heart because of your love.

Love is patient and kind. Love is not jealous or boastful or proud or rude. It does not demand its own way. It is not irritable and keeps no record of being wrong. It does not rejoice about injustice but rejoices whenever the truth wins out. Love never gives up, never loses faith, is always hopeful, and endures through every circumstance.
–1 Corinthians 13:4–7 NLT

I feel led to write on this again. Love is a very special thing God gives us because we must have God in our heart to truly love. It is the only way we can walk in love in this world. Love is patient and kind; we are to lift people up, not put them down. We are not to be jealous, boastful, or rude. Instead, we should be humble in every way. Love does not demand its own way; instead, it should help others find their way. It is not irritable and keeps no record of being wronged. We should think about others before ourselves. Love does not rejoice about injustice but rejoices whenever the truth wins out. Love never gives up, never loses faith, is always hopeful, and endures through every circumstance. Love is an amazing thing, and if you truly follow how God tells us to live in love, it will last for an eternity. We see it written before our eyes in God's Word, yet we cannot do it on our own. We need God to help us every step of the way through the Holy Spirit.

My prayer is that you truly learn to love all people, like God tells us. That you continue showing this world the love of Jesus Christ living in your heart. That everything you say and the way you act bring great honor and glory to God. I believe that if we live like this, our world would be a greater place to be.

Honor Marriage

Give honor to marriage, remain faithful. God will surely judge people who are immoral and those who commit adultery.
—Hebrews 13:4 NLT

I personally understand this more today. I have had two failed marriages because I was not the Christian man I claimed to be. Just like most of us, I knew God, but what I wanted was more important than what God wanted at the time. I did some good things and a lot of bad things. I was very prideful and selfish and had little love for others in my heart. I had a lot of love for what made me happy. Until we truly accept God through Jesus Christ's blood, we can't fully understand what real love is. Only through reading the Bible and understanding how we should treat others will we know true sacrificial love, which means putting others before our own selfish wants and needs (1 Corinthians 13:4–7).

Do we really understand what love fully is? It is sad to say most of us still have no clue what love is until God gives it to us. Sex is not love; it is lust. Love can only come through God. Marriage is a very special relationship that God puts together for a man and woman. God binds them together as one with him as the head. That is why it is so important to keep God first in your relationship. The man should put his wife before himself, and the woman should put her husband before herself, while doing everything to honor God. God's Word tells us that we should build a relationship on friendship first, then comes love, then comes marriage, and after the marriage comes lovemaking.

I know this world says that sex is love. This world tells us to start the relationship with sex, and if you like it, you try building a friendship. Then if both of you like it, you get married. That is completely opposite of God's Word. Living like this leads us to immoral living and adultery, which God will judge us for. Without God, you cannot have true love. You can have lust but not love, because God is love.

My prayer is that you have a strong relationship with God so you can have love in your heart and love for others, even the hard-to-love ones. That way, you can have a great relationship with your spouse built on love, with God as the head of the relationship.

Peace

I am leaving you with a gift—peace of mind and heart. And the peace I give is a gift the world cannot give. So, don't be troubled or afraid.
—John 14:27 NLT

The Lord continues talking to me about peace, so I must ask you this question: when you lay your head down to go to sleep at night, do you have peace? Seriously, take a moment to think about it. What keeps you up worrying at night? Material possessions, career choices, relatives, bills, this world, and Satan keep us from having peace. Jesus tells us that he gives us peace of mind and heart. He goes on to tell us this world cannot give us peace. When we continue putting our trust in this polluted world, we will not have peace. The only way you can have peace in this sorrowful world is to put your trust in Jesus! We need to remember that if we have doubts, fear, and worry, we are putting our trust in this world. If you want to lay your head down at night in peace, you need to put your trust in Jesus.

> When I am afraid, I put my trust in you. (Psalm 56:3)

> Trust in the Lord with all your heart. (Proverbs 3:5–6)

My prayer for you tonight is that when you lay your head down to sleep, you have great peace because you are putting your trust in Jesus Christ. Amen.

Separation

God put it in my heart to write about separation and why it keeps us from growing with him. When I was seven and a half years old, my dad and mom moved us from Boynton Beach to Summerfield. It doesn't seem much to the world, but to me, it was the end of the world. My grandmother was my rock. I spent most of my days with her, and she would take me and my brothers everywhere, including church. That is when I accepted Jesus Christ as my Savior. But when my family moved me from my grandmother to Summerfield, two things happened. The first thing I did was close my heart to all people. I would like them, but I would not love them in my heart; that way, I would never get hurt again. I know it sounds crazy, but that is what a seven-and-a-half-year-old boy did. That is exactly what I did; and worst of all, I blamed my mom, which put a wall between us.

It's crazy to think a seven-and-a-half-year-old kid would do that, but it happens every day to children everywhere. Not that their parents did anything wrong, but it's just the way we think. My life was never the same after that. I had lots of relationships with people, but I would never let them in my heart so I would not get hurt again. Slowly my life was getting darker because I was dying inside, and this was because I had no love in my heart. My life looked great from the outside to the world. But it really was a mess. I couldn't keep a relationship because I did not know how to love.

Then it came time for God to take my grandma home. To say I was not happy with God is an understatement. To tell you the truth, I hated God. I could not believe that God would take my grandmother away from me. She showed everybody her love for God through everything she did and said, and she was my rock. So my world started spiraling downhill fast. I was drinking and doing whatever I could do to fill that hole in my heart, only to make it even emptier. I chased after anything this world had to offer, trying to fill that hole in my heart. Yet I continued to die more and more each day.

I was now in my early twenties and thought that only getting married would fill my heart. Just like most of us, I felt I would do anything to try to feel that emptiness of not belonging. We got married, and a couple of years later, we were blessed to have a son. You would think that would fill the hole in my heart. I spent another thirty years and went through another failed marriage, only to figure out what truly was wrong with me. It doesn't matter what you try to fill that hole with; nothing will fill that void.

What I found out only a couple of years ago was that the separation as a child had built a wall around my heart, and I wasn't letting anybody in, not even Jesus. That is why, on discipleship walk 30 of Central Florida, at the table of James, our Lord Jesus spoke to me and asked me when I was going to allow him to break down that wall I had around my heart and allow him in and change the way I think. My life changed that day, and as I reflect today, we all have two problems. First, we're trying to fill that hole in our life with worldly things, and second, we have built a wall around our heart to protect ourselves.

We are born with that hole in our heart, and the older we get, the bigger the hole grows. That hole can only be filled by accepting a relationship with God through Jesus Christ. See, God created each one of us for a personal relationship with him, and until we accept that relationship, we have the hole in our heart because we're separated from him. We don't understand that it is a real relationship we desire to have. And because God wants it to be a real relationship, we have to accept it; he won't force it on us.

Now, with that said, God will put roadblocks in our life to show us that we need him. And it's only through that relationship that we can learn how to truly love. God is love, and without God, we cannot love.

We are New

Since you have heard about Jesus and have learned the truth that comes from him, throw off your sinful nature and your former way of life, which is corrupted by lust and deception. Instead, let the spirit renew your thoughts and attitudes. Put on your new nature, created to be like God—truly righteous and holy.
—Ephesians 4:21–24 NLT

When we accept Jesus Christ as our Lord and Savior, we receive the Holy Spirit in our hearts. We have been made new in the Holy Spirit, so we need to put away our old sinful nature and follow God. We should have new thoughts and attitudes like God's, which are righteous and holy. We have to remember our body no longer belongs to us; it belongs to God, and we need to treat our body as the holy temple it is. We should take care of our body and watch what we put in it and how we use it. From the food we eat to the language we use and the thoughts we allow in, everything should show others the love of Jesus Christ living in our heart, bringing honor and glory to God.

My prayer is that you throw out your sinful body and put on your new heavenly body. All our thoughts and attitudes are to honor God. I pray that you live a life that is righteous and pleasing to God in everything you do and say.

We Aren't Worldly

For you are not a true Jew just because you were born of Jewish parents or because you have gone through the ceremony of circumcision. No, a true Jew is one whose heart is right with God. And a true circumcision is not merely obeying the letter of the law, rather, it is a change of heart produced by the spirit. And the person with the changed heart seeks praise from God, not people.
—Romans 2:28–29 NLT

Please take time to read these verses again. This is most of us, including me. We are trying to do everything to please people and trying to fit in instead of doing what pleases God. I knew God, but I was trying to do everything I could to fit into this world. Only when life brought me to my knees and I looked up did I see the truth. When I had a change in my life, I accepted Jesus Christ as my Savior in my head. I never accepted the heart change—period. It is sad that it took me fifty-two years to figure that out. I was trying to do everything on my own for fifty-two years. I had accepted Jesus Christ's salvation, but I was still missing something in my heart. That is why I was still trying to please this dark world. But at fifty-two years old, at a disciple walk in Central Florida, at the table of James (that's what it was called), my life drastically changed. I heard our Lord ask me, "When are you going to allow me to break down that wall you have around your heart, come into your heart, and change the way you think?"

Brothers and sisters, my life began to change that moment! That is when I started doing everything to please God because of my love. I was the one keeping the change from happening, not allowing Jesus Christ to come into my heart and change the way that I think.

My prayer is that you allow Jesus to come into your heart, your mind, and your body to change the way you think. Then you will want to do everything to please God because of your love for him.

True Love

Dear friends, let us continue to love one another, for love comes from God. Anyone who loves is a child of God and knows God. But anyone who does not love does not know God, for God is love.
—1 John 4:7–8 NLT

See, we cannot truly love without God, because God is love. We can lust without God, but we cannot love. I want you to really take some time to think about this. God even had Paul write a whole chapter about what love is, as is found in 1 Corinthians 13.

The Strength Of Love

Love is patient and kind. Love is not jealous or boastful or proud or rude. It does not demand its own way. It is not irritable, and it keeps no record of being wrong. It does not rejoice about injustice but rejoices whenever the truth wins out. Love never gives up, never loses faith, is always hopeful, and endures through every circumstance.
—1 Corinthians 14:4–7 NLT

Love is why we have great faith. Love is why we can love when others cannot. Love is why we do the things we do. Love is why we follow God and keep his commandments. Love is why we continue to love others when they have given up or are unlovable in our eyes. Love is why we can forgive. Love is why we live a life that shows the world the love of Jesus Christ living inside our heart. We must show people we love God in the way we speak and in our actions, which brings great glory to God.

My prayer is that you truly want to grow your love, then you can follow God and keep his commandments. That way, you'll be able to love all people in such a way that it shows this world the love God put in each one of us. Love lives inside your heart through his Holy Spirit.

Grow A True Relationship

Don't worry about anything instead, pray about everything. Tell God what you need and thank him for all that he has done. Then you will experience God's peace, which exceeds anything we can understand. His peace will guard your heart and mind as you live in Jesus Christ.
—Philippians 4:6–7 NLT

Our Lord put it in my heart to ask this question: When you lay your head down to sleep, do you have true peace in your heart? I have been reflecting on my past, especially the last seven years! I have struggled and fought for fifty-two years of my life to have peace every day and failed miserably. I was trying to do it all on my own, all because of my pride. I believed I could handle it, that it was too small or not that important to ask God for help. Boy, how wrong I was. God had to humble me and help me see I needed Him every second of the day, not just when I thought I needed his help or whenever I felt like I was in way over my head, drowning.

I finally understood what it meant when the Lord asked me to let him break down the wall I had built around my heart and allow him to change the way I think. My heart was so hardened by a childhood experience, and I carried the pain through the years. I wasn't the nicest person and certainly far from being like Jesus Christ.

Our Heavenly Father wants us to have a real relationship with Jesus Christ, who is living inside our heart, that helps change the way we think. When you realize it, that is when you have true peace. Not that you won't still have hills and valleys in life, but you will have strength in your heart knowing Jesus Christ is with you through those hills and valleys to mold you with the Holy Spirit to be more like Jesus Christ. I'm not saying this will happen overnight; it took me another seven years (after allowing him in) to soften my hardened heart to have this true peace. I also had to do my part to grow my relationship by reading God's Word, praying, listening to the Holy Spirit, and giving God well-deserved praise.

I mentioned before WRAP: wrap your heart around Jesus!

>	*W*rite a verse down from God's Word.
>	*R*ead the verse again.
>	*A*pply it to your life.
>	*P*ray about it.

My prayer is that you wrap your heart around Jesus Christ so you can be the light in this dark world, that exceeds anything we can understand.

Show Time

Instead, be kind to each other, tender hearted, forgiving one another, just as God through Christ has forgiven you.
—Ephesians 4:31 NLT

We should be showing the world how to live a righteous, godly life by being an example to them and showing the love of Jesus Christ shining through our hearts into everything we speak, do, and say in such a way that it brings great honor and glory to God. I want you to really think about that. If everything you do and say always brings pleasure and contentment to God, then you truly are living a godly life, and you are ready for the moment when God calls you home. You will always be tenderhearted and forgiving toward others because the love of Jesus Christ is beaming from you.

The other thing is you attain great, calming peace in your life because you know God is with you every step of the way on your path to righteousness. The King of kings has gone before you and won this war.

> So be strong and courageous! Do not be afraid and do not panic before them. For the Lord your God will personally go ahead of you. He will neither fail you nor abandon you. (Deuteronomy 31:6 NLT)

I pray that you are showing this world the love of Jesus Christ in your heart and that it brings pride and satisfaction to God.

Give It to God

And so, dear brothers and sisters, I plead with you to give your bodies to God because of all he has done for you. Let them be a living and holy sacrifice—the kind he will find acceptable. This is truly the way to worship him.
—Romans 12:1 NLT

Remember, Jesus Christ gave his body over for our sins because of his love. That is why I can't understand how people cannot give their whole life over to God. Some of you will give 50, 60, 70, or even 90 percent. Only very few will give 100 percent of their life over to Jesus Christ. Some of you who are only giving God 90 percent or less wonder why God is not answering your prayers. I will admit 90 percent is a lot, but did Jesus only give up 90 percent of his body on the cross for you? No, he gave his whole body up for you. Brothers and sisters, that is love.

I ask you this question: Who do you love more, God or yourself? Do you truly want to see God answer your prayers and use you more than you could ever imagine? You need to give your whole body over to God; that way, you will be acceptable and pleasing to God. Then God will be able to use you to do amazing things and answer your prayers because you will be following his will for your life.

> I know all the things you do, that you are neither hot nor cold. I wish that you were one or the other! But since you are like lukewarm water, neither hot nor cold, I will spit you out of my mouth! (Revelation 3:15–16)

God is never wishy-washy or confused. He is the same today as yesterday and in the time of our grandparents. God's words will never change. God doesn't make mistakes, and he definitely means what he says.

My prayers are that you give your whole body to Christ; that way, God will be able to use you to do amazing things, and he will answer your prayers.

The Love Of Your Father

Our Lord has put in my heart to tell you how much he loves you and to ask you this question: How much do you love God? More than your sinful ways? Do you love God so much that you tell others about his Son, Jesus Christ? Do your actions toward others bring honor to or glorify God? If you would, please take a few minutes and ask yourself again, "Do I really trust and love God?"

> Love is patient and kind. Love is not jealous or boastful or proud or rude. It does not demand its own way. It is not irritable, and it keeps no record of being wronged. It does not rejoice about injustice but rejoices whenever the truth wins out. Love never gives up, never loses faith, is always hopeful, and the endures through every circumstance. (1 Corinthians 13:4–7 NLT)

Brothers and sisters, God loves you even more than words can express.

> What is the price of five sparrows—two copper coins? Yet God does not forget a single one of them. "And the very hairs on your head are all numbered. So don't be afraid; you are more valuable than a whole flock of sparrows." (Luke 12:6–7 NLT)

That is why God created every one of us. God loves you and wants to have an eternal relationship with you. So why don't you love him in the same way?

No One Can Separate Us from God's Love

No power in the sky or in the earth below—indeed, nothing in all creation will ever be able to separate us from the love of God that is revealed in Christ Jesus our Lord.
—Romans 8:39 NLT

It is so true; nothing in this world can separate us from the love of God. God sent his love through his Son, Jesus Christ. In turn, Jesus showed us love by being a sacrifice and dying for our sins. I pray you realize God created you and that you are so very special to him. He wants you to have an eternal relationship with him because of his love. It is your choice if you accept that relationship through Jesus Christ. That is why it is a true relationship. Jesus Christ is always with you through the Holy Spirit, and you may choose to turn from him. However, as soon as you repent and turn back, Jesus Christ is waiting with open arms. Brothers and sisters, you will never find love like this on earth, a love so strong it lasts for eternity.

> God saved you by his grace when you believed. And you can't take credit for this; it is a gift from God. Salvation is not a reward for the good things we have done, so none of us can boast about it. For we are God's masterpiece. He has created

us anew in Christ Jesus, so we can do the good things he planned for us long ago. (Ephesians 2:8–10 NLT)

My prayers are that you really understand how much Jesus Christ loves you.

What About Me

One of the criminals hanging beside him scoffed, "So you're the Messiah, are you? Prove it by saving yourself—and us, too, while you're at it!" But the other criminal protested, "Don't you fear God even when you have been sentenced to death? We deserve to die for our crimes, but this man hasn't done anything wrong." Then he said, "Jesus, remember me when you come into your kingdom." And Jesus replied, "I assure you today, you will be with me in paradise."
—Luke 23:39–43 NLT

We see in these verses one thief went with Jesus to paradise; the other one did not. Why? We are told that we must do one thing or another to get into heaven with God, but this thief had done nothing. Or had he? Let me explain with God's Word.

> For the wages of sin is death, but the gift of God is eternal life through Christ Jesus our Lord. (Romans 6:23 NLT)

We must understand that it is a gift from God. We cannot earn it. We cannot do good works to receive it. We also cannot buy it. Nobody can do it for us. You must do it for yourself. What must we do to accept this free gift from God through Jesus Christ? It is easy but hard. Let me explain more with God's Word.

> For this is how God loved the world: He gave his one and only Son, so that everyone who believes

in him will not perish but have eternal life. (John 3:16 NLT)

For I am not ashamed of this Good News about Christ. It is the power of God at work, saving everyone who believes—the Jew first and also the Gentiles. This Good News tells us how God makes us right in his sight. This is accomplished from start to finish by faith. As the Scriptures say, "It is through faith that a righteous person has life." (Romans 1:16–18 NLT)

The first thief said, "If you are the Messiah, prove it by saving yourself and us too." He thought, *Just in case, I will believe.*

The second thief asked the first thief, "Don't you believe in God?" Then he went on to tell the first thief that they deserved what they were getting because of what they had done. Then he said, "This man [Jesus] is innocent." He asked Jesus, "Remember me when you come into your kingdom."

Jesus said, "Today you will be with me in paradise."

The second thief admitted he was wrong and had faith that Jesus was the Messiah. Plain and simple, the first thief was doing it just in case Jesus was the Messiah; he was being a bit sarcastic, I feel. The first thief just had a head change. The second thief believed in God. He also admitted he was a sinner and needed Jesus. The second thief had a heart change and had faith that Jesus was who he said he was. That is why he asked Jesus to remember him. It is by our faith in believing Jesus is the Son of God that makes us right in God's eyes.

My prayers are that through your faith, you believe that Jesus is the Son of God. That is what makes you right with God.

Change Me

Today I would like to share something God laid on my heart to say. I used to pray all the time for God to change all the people I thought were wrong, and that was just about everybody. One day, I was standing in front of the mirror, and God opened my eyes; it was not everybody with the problems. It was me! The only thing I could change was me. So don't complain about a person; help them. Don't say stuff behind their back; love them. Give love, not hate. Keep this in mind: the one with the most toys doesn't win. It's the one who has the most love in their heart for all people. When you are standing before Jesus Christ on the day of judgment, ask Jesus if he loves all your toys or if he cares about all the people you have shown love to. I don't know about you, but I'm thankful for Jesus for showing me what love is and the ability to love all people, especially the lost.

Sins of the Heart

And then he added, "It is what comes from inside that defiles you. For from within, out of a person's heart, evil thoughts, sexual immorality, theft, murder, adultery, greed, wickedness, deceit, lustful desires, envy, slander, pride and foolishness. All these vile things come from within, they are what defile you."
—Mark 7:20–23 NLTs

We must understand that all this comes from our old sinful heart. It was our sinful nature to sin, but now that we have truly repented of those sins and turned to Jesus Christ, our old sinful heart has died and been reborn with a new heart from Jesus. We no longer want to sin or chase after this sinful world; instead, we now choose to follow Jesus Christ and show this world the light of Jesus Christ living in our heart. Everything we do and speak should bring light to others in the darkness of their sins. We should be helping our brothers and sisters win their battles with sin, not cut them down or disparage them.

> Sing for joy, O heavens! Rejoice, O earth! Burst into song, O mountains! For the Lord has comforted his people and will have compassion on them in their suffering. (Isaiah: 49:13 NLT)

My prayer is that you are aware of your sins, turn away from them, and fill your heart with the love of Jesus so that you now want to show this world the love of Jesus Christ living in your heart and everything you do and say in such a way that it brings great honor and glory to God.

What Was Missing

Have you ever wondered why you feel like you are missing something? When we are born, we are missing something; and the older we get, the more that hole in our heart grows. We try filling it with the things of this world and only feel emptier and more lost. My friends, it is because we are missing a relationship with God. God created each one of us to have a special relationship with us; only God can fill that hole in our heart. The only way we can have God in our heart is to accept his Son, *Jesus Christ*, as our Lord and Savior. When we accept Jesus Christ, God sends Jesus to live in us through the Holy Spirit to live in our heart. That is when our heart starts filling with God's love because it is a true relationship; we must do our part by reading God's Word, praying, and listening to the Holy Spirit.

My prayers are that you have accepted Jesus Christ as your Lord and Savior fully inside your heart. Remember to *wrap* your heart around God by reading God's Word, the Bible; praying; and listening to the Holy Spirit as he guides your life through this world and fills your heart with God's love for all people, especially the lost.

How To Grow—W. R. A. P.

How do we grow our relationship with God? We do it through reading God's Word, praying, and listening to the Holy Spirit. I have learned the best way to grow that relationship with God is by wrapping our heart around God, and this is how I learned to do it.

>*W*rite a verse down from God's Word.
>*R*ead the verse again.
>*A*pply the verse to your life.
>*P*ray about it.

This is how we grow our own personal relationship with God through Jesus Christ. I have been doing it for the last seven years, and it has changed my life. I promise, if you do it, it will change your life.

First Twelve Apostles

The following are the apostles who walked three years with Jesus:

1. Simon (whom he named Peter)
2. Andrew (Peter's brother)
3. James
4. John
5. Philip
6. Bartholomew
7. Matthew
8. Thomas
9. James (son of Alphaeus)
10. Simon (who was called the zealot)
11. Judas (son of James)
12. Judas Iscariot (who later betrayed him)

About the Author

Shanon Crouch was born in Post Falls, Idaho, and raised in Marion County, Florida. He was raised in a Christian home with his brothers and sisters. He was first saved at seven and a half years of age.

He attended Lake Worth High School, where he was very active in 4-H and Future Farmers of America. He also attended trade schools for John Deere and CAT heavy equipment companies. His thirty-nine-year career as a certified top mechanic served him well. His other interest was football, where he coached both middle and high school teams.

He has two children and three grandsons. He is married to his beautiful faith partner, Joyce. They live in East Tennessee, on a small farm.

Shanon as a child was always ready to jump into whatever he thought would be exciting just to say he did it. This would lead him to be more worldly than Christian. He claimed to be a Christian and was active in churches throughout his adult life. He was very good at coaching and would have his teams pray before games as well as give them good godly advice for young adults; however, his actions did not reflect the godly advice he was giving.

He was a Wednesday or Sunday church Christian. In church, he acted as expected. The rest of the week, he was living the life of the world—drinking, cussing, telling dirty jokes. He eventually found himself angry, not happy, and with two failed marriages. He didn't want to be around family or good friends.

Two things happened that would turn him back to serving God. One of his brothers-in-law and best friends, Brian Mayo, called him out on his behavior to the family and his actions. The other was his diagnosis of prostate cancer, stage 4, and during the operation, another issue developed that caused the second major surgery within twenty-four hours. He would become septic, spend nine days in the ICU and seventeen days in the hospital, and go home with months of recovery, unable to work. This opened his real relationship with God. At the age of fifty-two, he had promised God that if he recovered, he would be his humble servant for life.

That was the start of Shanon's change of life. He is now coaching discipleship and Celebrate Recovery Ministry (CR) as well as WRAP (Wrap Your Heart around God) to teach how to understand and grow your relationship with God.

John 13:35 NLT—"Your love for one another will prove to the world that you are my disciples"—is his daily goal.